ALBERT

Albert

AND THE

y el

MILK PAIL

Cubo d leche

JAN HAHN

ILLUSTRATED BY TRACY FOSTER   TRANSLATED BY ASHLEY WILLIAMS

Parson's Porch Books

Albert and the Milk Pail
ISBN: Softcover 978-1-960326-21-8
Copyright © 2023 by Jan Hahn

Parson's Porch Books is an imprint of Parson's Porch & Company (PP&C) in Cleveland, Tennessee. PP&C is a self-funded charity which earns money by publishing books of noted authors, representing all genres. Its face and voice is **David Russell Tullock** who you can contact at: dtullock@parsonsporch.com.

Parson's Porch & Company *turns books into bread & milk* by sharing its profits with the poor.

www.parsonsporch.com

DEDICATED TO

DR. LAURA HOPFER &
DR. WILLIAM RUSSELL

WHOSE LOVE AND ENTHUSIASM FOR TEACHING

INSPIRED US TO NEVER GIVE UP.

Dedicado a
los Doctores Laura Hopfer &
William Russell

cuyo amor e entusiasmo de enseñanza nos

inspird a rendimos nunca.

CHAPTER ONE

ONCE UPON A TIME THERE LIVED A LITTLE FROG NAMED ALBERT

Érase una vez, vivió una rana pequefta nombrada Albert.

ALBERT LIVED IN A BOG.

Albert vivia en un pantano.

Behind the woods,

altrás del bosque,

NEXT TO A FARM

al lado de una granja.

LIFE WAS GOOD FOR ALBERT. HE LIVED WITH HIS FAMILY. THERE WAS HIS FATHER ADAM AND MOTHER EVE AND HIS BROTHER CALEB, DEVON, ELWIN, AND FRITZ AND HIS SISTERS EWEN, HARRIET, INGRID, AND JASMINE.

La vida era muy buena para Albert. Se vivia con su familia. Habian un padre Adam y madre Eve y su hermanos Caleb, Devon, Elwin, y Fritz y su hermanas Gwen, Harriet, Ingrid, y Jasmine.

EVERY DAY HE WENT TO SCHOOL WHERE HE LEARNED WHAT ALL FROGS NEED TO KNOW: HOW TO SIT ON A LILY PAD.

Todos los dias él se fue a la escuela donde aprendio lo que necesitan saber todas las ranas: como sentarse bien sobre una almohadilla del lirio.

How to catch Flies and

como agarrar moscas, y

How to croak in tune

Como croar en sintonia

EVERY NIGHT. HIS MOTHER PREPARE THE MOST DELICIOUS MEALS:

FLY SOUP,

Todas las noches, su mama preparó las comidas más deliciosas:

sopa de moscas,

Fly Burgers, and best of all Fly Pizza

Hambourguesa de moscas, y
major que todo,
pizza de moscas.

After dinner, Albert's mother would tuck all her children into their beds and read a story until they fell fast asleep.

Después de cenar, la mama de Albert se metia a todas su niñios en sus camas y les leaba un cuento o poema hasta se dormian todos.

One evening, as the sun was setting and shadows raced across the land, Albert's mother noticed that he was not in bed.

Una noche, mientras el sol empezó a caer y sombras extendieron sobre la tierra, la mama de Albert notó que él no estaba en SU cama!

WHERE IS ALBERT? HE IS SO CURIOUS ABOUT THINGS HE SOMETIME LOSES TRACK OF TIME." SO ALBERT'S MOTHER LOOKED AND LOOKED. SHE LOOKED IN THE LIBRARY. NO ALBERT!

"Donde está Albert? Él es tan curioso de/sobre cosas que a veces pierde la nocion del tiempo." Entonces su mama buscó y buscó y buscó. Ella buscó en la biblioteca. No estuvo Albert!

She looked in her husband's workshop. No Albert!

Ella buscó en el taller de su esposo. No Albert!

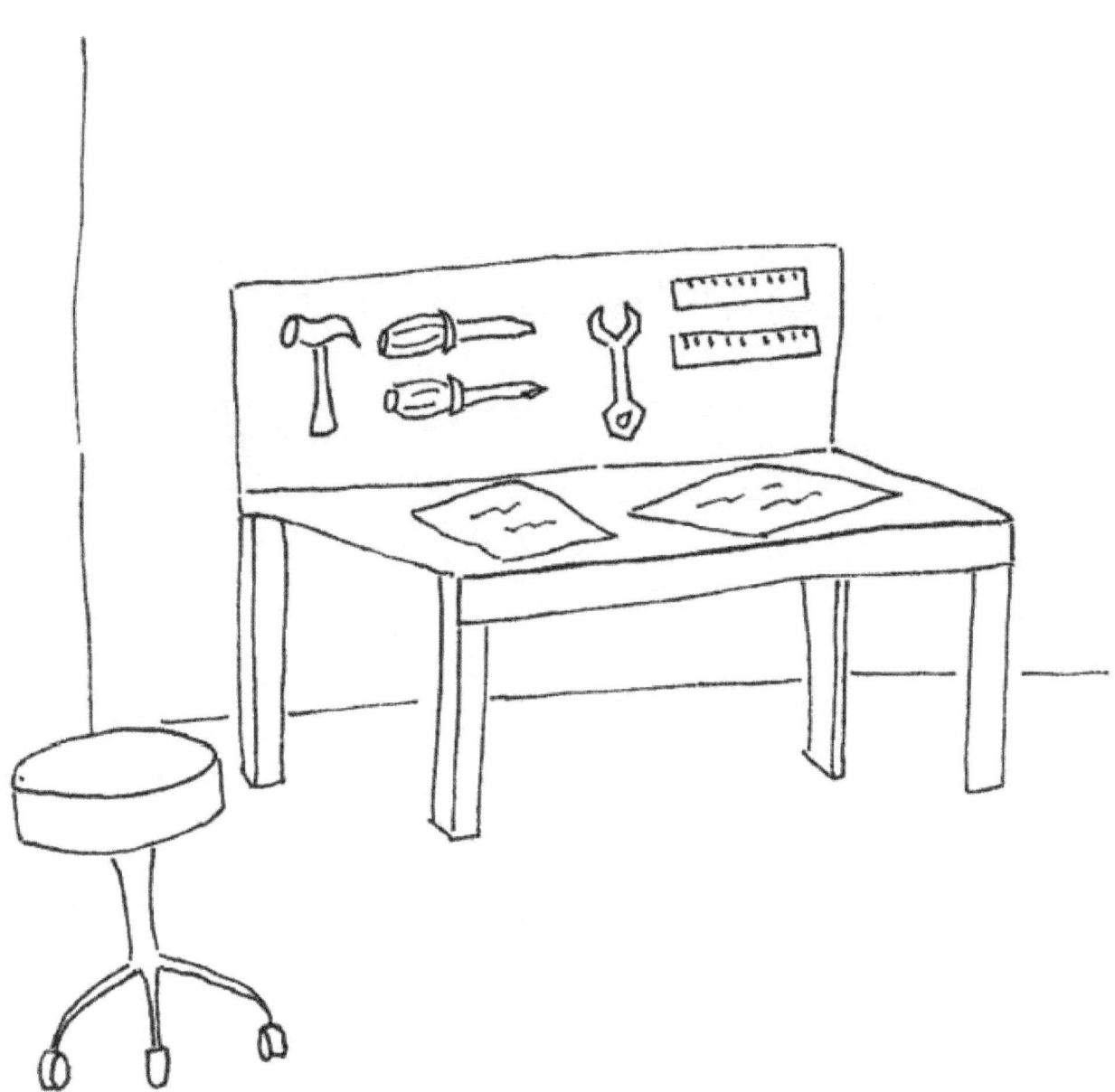

She even looked in Albert's secret hiding place which Albert thought no one knew about. No Albert!

También buscó en el escondite secreto de Albert que él penso nadie conocia. No Albert!

NIGHT HAD NOW FALLED AND ALBERT'S FAMILY HAD BECOME FRANTIC FOR IT WAS TERRIBLY DARK. SHE SUMMONED HER HUBAND AND ALL EIGHT BROTHERS AND SISTERS AND FOR THE NEXT NEXT HOUR, THEY SEARCHED EVERYWHERE THEY COULD IMAGINE ALBERT COULD BE, BUT NO ALBERT!

La noche hubo caido ahora y su mama se pusó frenetica porque fue terriblemente oscuro. Ella convocó a su esposo y todos del ocho hermanos y para la hora siguiente buscaron por todos lados donde podria estar Albert. Pero nada de Albert!

SO WHERE WAS ALBERT? AND WHAT WAS HE DOING??????

Por tanto donde fue Albert y que estaba hacienda?

ALBERT HAD DECIDED LATE THAT AFTERNOON TO HOP OVER TO THE FARM. HE HAD NEVER BEEN THERE BEFORE, AND HE THOUGHT IT WOULD BE AN EXCITING PLACE TO EXPLORE. AND IT CERTAINLY WAS! HE SAW COWS.

Albert habia decidido tarde esa tarde para saltar a la granja. Nunca habia estado allá antés y él pensaba que seria un lugar fascinante para explorar! Y por Seguro era!

El vio:vacas.

Chickens,

gallinas,

PIGS, AND

cerdos, y

HORSES.

caballos.

BUT THE MOST INTERESTING PLACE WAS THE BARN.

Pero el lugar más interesante
era el granero.

ALBERT SQUEEZED HIS WAY PAST THE BARN DOOR, AND AS HE LOOKED ABOUT, HE SAW A LARGE PAIL STANDING NEXT TO A STALL. THIS WAS CLEARLY SOMETHING THAT HE MUST CHECK OUT!

Albert se apretó su camino por delante de puerta del granero, y como él echó un vistazo, miro un cubo grande al lado de una casilla. Esta era, sin duda, algo que él debia investigar!

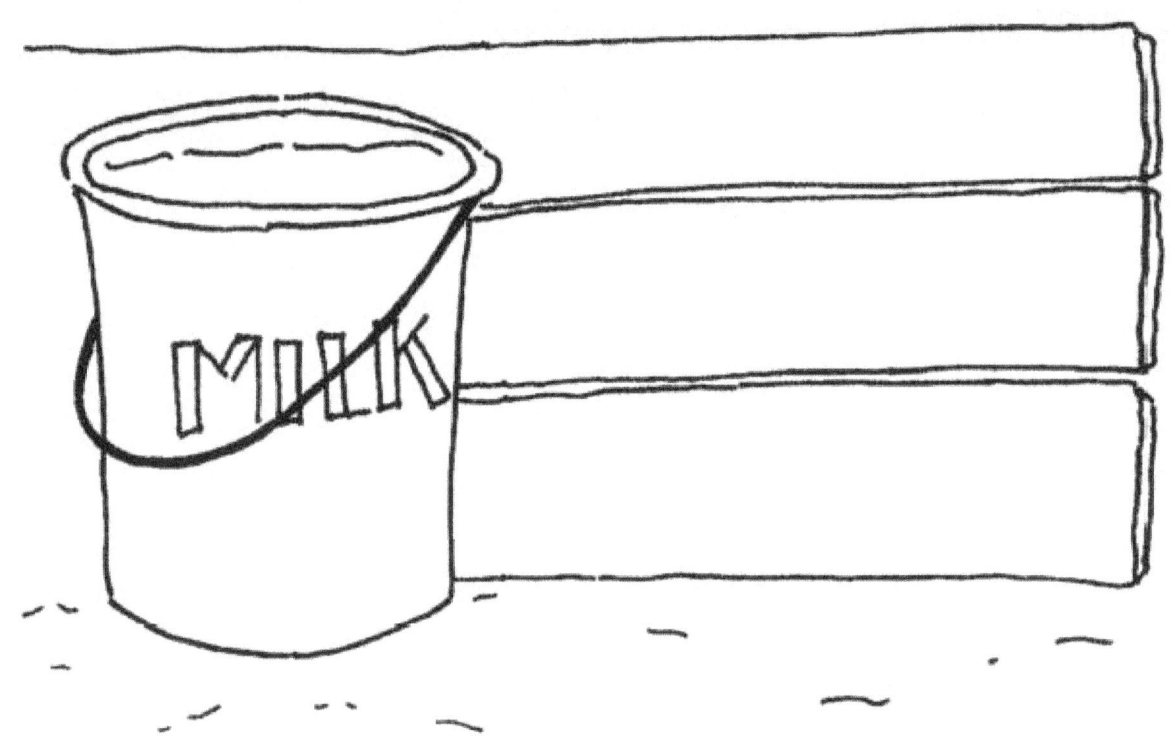

SINCE HE WAS TOO SMALL TO PEER OVER THE EDGE, ALBERT CLIMBED THE GUARDRAIL AND SLOWLY INCHED HIS WAS ALONG UNTIL HE COULD LEAN BACKWARDS, HOLDING TIGHTLY TO THE TOP RAIL, AND LOOKED OVER HIS BACK INTO THE BUCKET.

Como era demasiado pequeñio para atisbar por encima el horde, Albert subió a la baranda y avancio lentamente hasta que él pudiera apoyarse hasta atrás, agarrando firmamente a la parte de arriba de la barranda, y miró hacia atras en el cubo.

SUDDENLY HE SNEEZED AND BEFORE HE KNOW WHAT WAS HAPPENING, HE HAD TUMBLED "HEAD OVER HEELS" INTO THE PAIL AND IT WAS FILLED WITH MILK!

De repente, él estomudio y antes que él notó lo que pasaba, él habia caida "cabeza sobre tacones" en el cubo. Era lleno con leche!

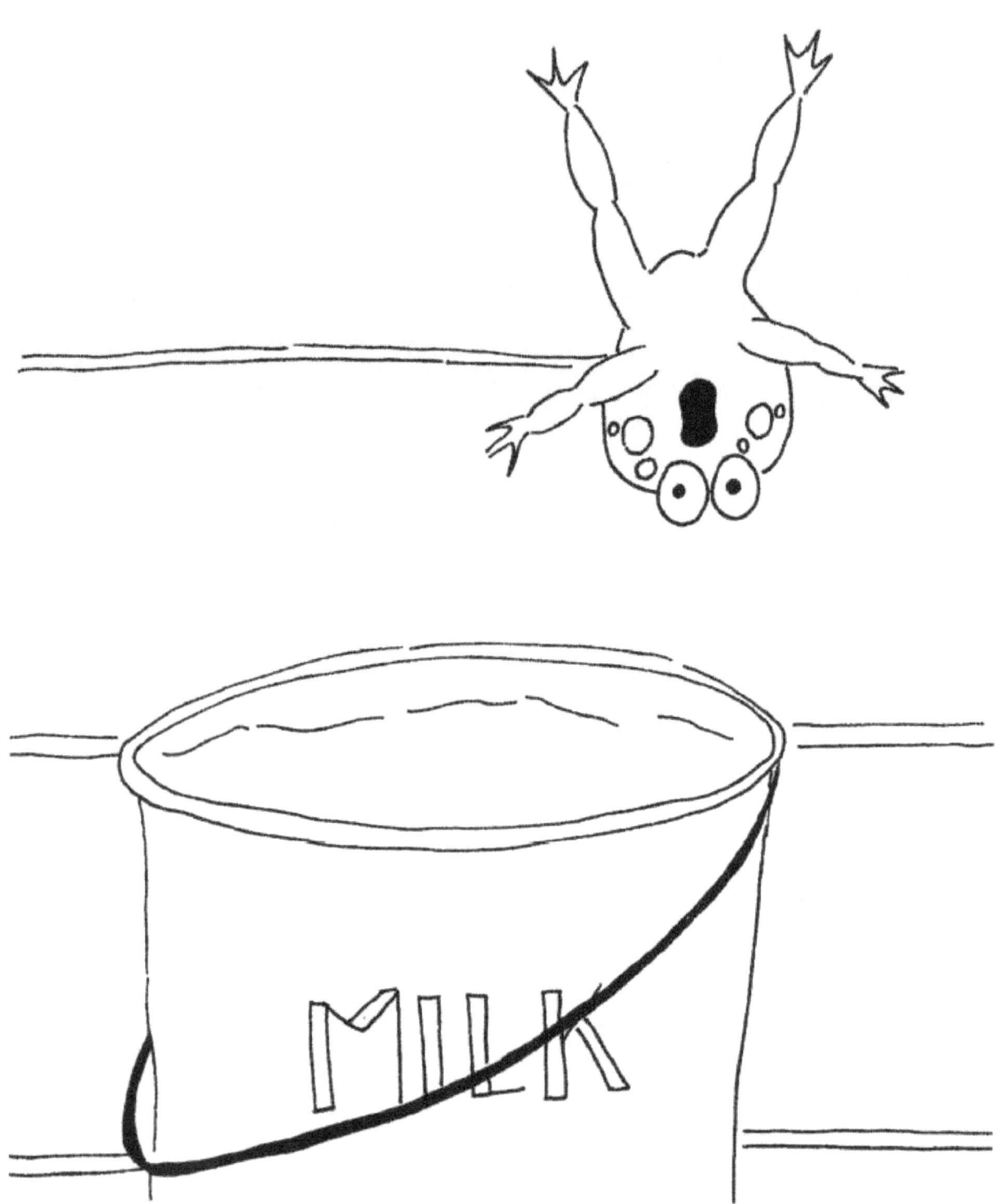

IT TOOK A FEW MINUTES FOR ALBERT OT GET HIS BEARING BUT WHEN HE DID, HE DISCOVERED IT WAS VERY EASY TO SWIM IN MILK. HE COULD DO A BACKSTROKE.

Le costaba algunos minutos para orientarle pero cuando le orientó, el descubrió que era muy facil nadar en leche. El podia nadar a espalda,

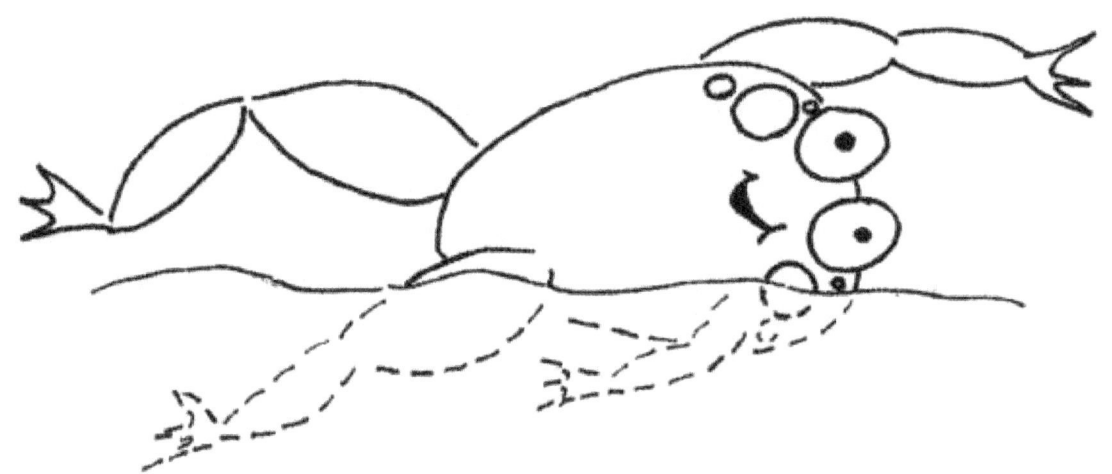

THE AUSTRALIAN CRAWL, AND

el rastreo de Australia, y

EVEN THE BREASTSTROKE.

también nadir a braza.

BEST OF ALL, HE COULD DRINK

AS MUCH AS HE WANTED.

Mejor que todo, el podia tomar
toda la leche que queria.

CHAPTER TWO

ALBERT PLAYED HAPPILY FOR ABOUT AN HOUR AND THEN HE DECIDED TO CLIMB OUT, BUT ALAS, EVERY TIME HE GRABBED HOLD OF THE BUCKET'S SIDES, HE SLIPPED BACK INTO THE MILK. TRY AS HE MIGHT, HE WAS UNABLE TO GET OUT. HE WAS TRAPPED, AND HE WAS GETTING VERY TIRED AND VERY SCARED.

Albert jugó alegremente para casi una hora y decidió subirse afuera. Pero por desgracia! Cada vez él intento a grabar al lado del cubo, se resbaló en la leche. Trato como podria el no podia salir. Era atrapado y se pusó muy cansado y asustado.

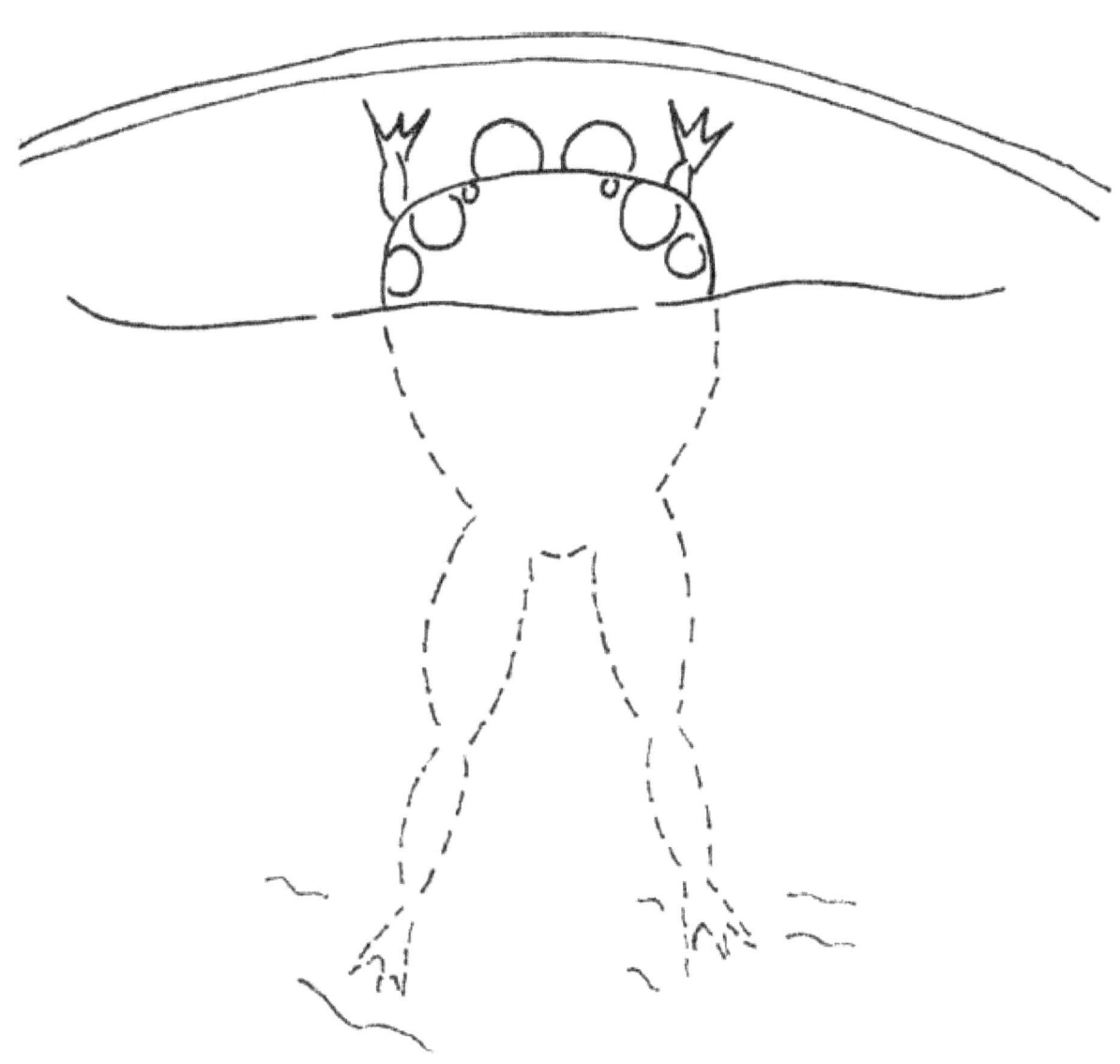

He call out the names of his family: Dad! Mom! Caleb! Devon! Elwin! Fritz! Ewen! Harriett! Ingrid! Jasmine!

El grito los nombres de su familia: Papa! Mama! Caleb! Devon! Elwin! Fritz! Gwen! Harriet! Ingrid! Jasmine!

No one heard. He was along and it was very dark and very quiet in the barn. Albert swam and swam and swam. After an hour, he became so tired he slipped below the surface of the milk. Poor Albert! His curiosity had gotten him into a predicament from which he could not escape. No one would every find him in time to rescue him.

Nadie le oyó. Él era solo y era muy oscuro y muy tranquilo en el granero. Albert nadó y nadó y nadó. Después de una hora, él se cansó tanto que se resbaló debajo de la superficie de la leche. Pobrecito! Su curiosidad le hubo puesto en un apuro del que no podria escapar. Nadie le encontraria en tiempo para salvarle.

Back at the house, Mr, and Mrs., Frog had become frantic with fear, The only thing they could do was to ask for help from all the inhabitants on the bog. First, they called the fireflies. After hearing the story, the fireflies flew into the sky and flashed for all to see a summons for assistance.

SAVE OUR SON

De regreso a la casa, Sr. y Sra. Rana se pusieron freneticos con temor. Lo unico que podian hacer era pedir ayuda de los habitantes del pantano. Primero llamaron a las luciemagas. Despues de escuchar el cuento, las luciemagas volaron hacia el cielo y destellaron para que todos podrian ver la citacion para ayuda.

Salve a nuestro hijo!

A POSSE OF 'POSSUMS ARRIVED.

Una banda de possums llego.

A TROOP OF FIELD MICE WITH THEIR SNIFFING BEETLES SOON APPEARED.

Un batallón de ratones del campo con sus escarabajos olfateando aparecieron pronto.

NIGHT OWLS CAME

Noctámbulos vinieron

THE CROWS FLOCKED IN.

Las comejas acudieron en masa.

EVEN THE BATS CAME TO HELP.

Hasta los murcielagos vinieron
para ayudar.

AFTER EVERYONE HAD BEEN GIVEN THEIR ORDERS, THE SEARCH BEGAN. ALL MR. AND MRS. FROG AND THEIR CHILDREN COULD DO NOW WAS WAIT AND PRAY AND PRAY AND PRAY.

Después de todos hubieron dado sus ordenes, la busqueda empezó. Sr. y Sra. Rana y su familia no pudieron hacer nada mas que esperar y orar, y orar, y orar.

BACK AT THE BARN, ALBERT WAS BEGINNING TO DROWN. HE THOUGHT OF HOW STUPID IT WAS TO HAVE HOPPED OVER TO THE BARN WITHOUT TELLING ANYONE WHERE HE WAS GOING. AND HOW STUPID IT HAD BEEN FOR HIM TO LEAD BACKWARDS OVER THE PAIL. HE WAS SO SAD THAT THIS WAS HOW HIS LIFE WAS GOING TO END AND THEN A LITTLE VOICE FROM DEEP WITHING HIS BRAIN SHOUTED OUT. "YOU ARE TOO YOUNG TO DIE! DON'T GIVE UP! AND ALBERT SWAM TO THE SURFACE AND ONE AGAIN TRIED TO SCALE THE SIDES OF THE PAIL.

De regreso al granero, Albert empezó ahogar. Él pensó acerca de como tonto era saltar hacia el granero sin mencionar a nadie a donde se iria. Y tan tonto era a inclinarse hacia atrás arriba del cubo. Éstuvo tan triste que esta fue la manera como su vida era terminar. Y luego una voz pequeña del profundo de su cerebro gritó. "Eres demasiado joven para morir. Note rindas!"
Y Albert nadó a la superficie y otra vez intentó subir al lado del cubo.

For over an hour, Albert struggled but eventually he tied and once again, he sank below the surface. Albert could only think of how much his family would miss him and he became very sad.

Más de una hora, Albert lucho pero finalmento él intentd y otra vez, se sumergió abajo de la superficie. Albert pudo pensar en nada más que como tanto su familia le extrañaria y se pusó muy triste.

SUDDENLY, THAT SAME LITTLE VOICE SHOUTED OUT. "YOU ARE TOO YOUNG TO DIE! DON'T GIVE UP!" AND ALBERT MUSTERED THE COURAGE AND STRENGTH TO SWIM TO THE SURFACE, AND ONCE AGAIN, THE TRIED TO SCALE THE SIDE OF THE PAIL.

De repente, esa voz pequeñia gritó. "Eres demasiado joven para morir! No te rindas!"

Albert hizo acopio de valor y fuerza para nadar a la superficie y otra vez él intentó subir al lado del cubo.

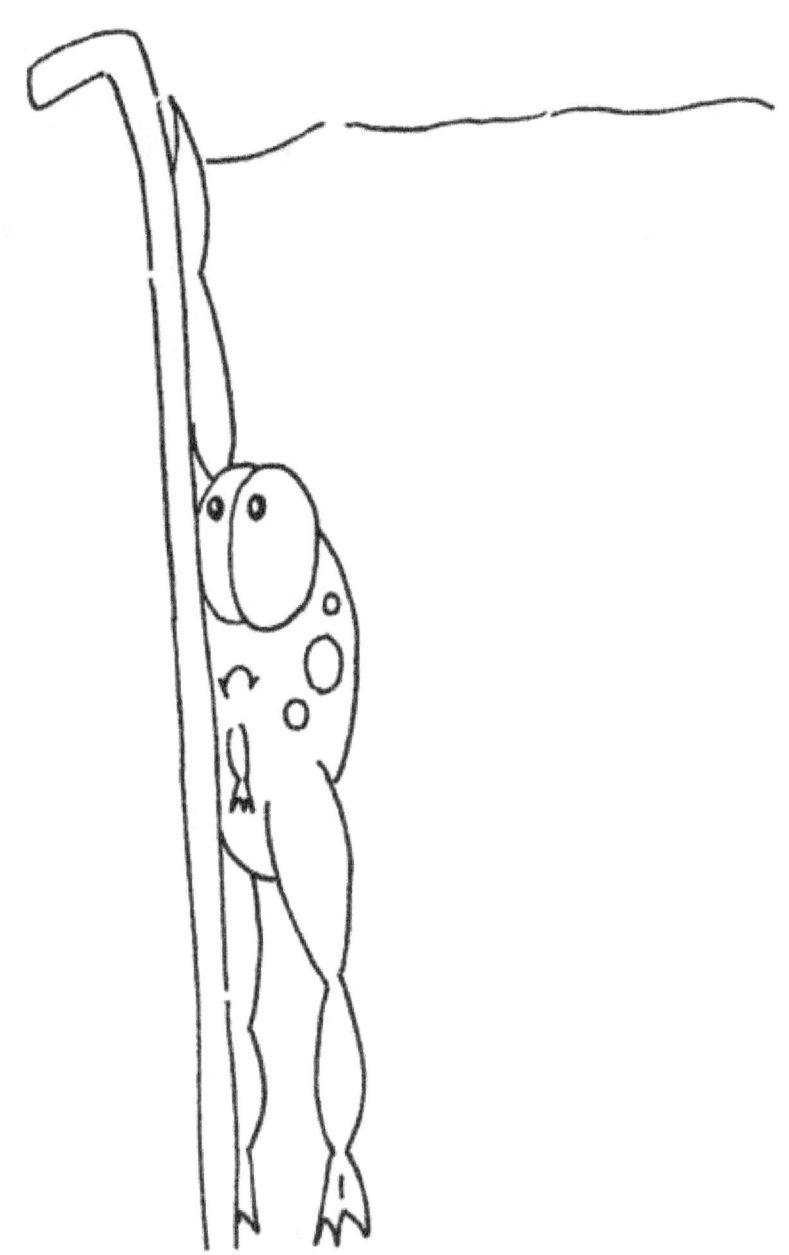

WHILE ALL THIS WAS GOING ON WITH ALBERT,
THE SEARCH TEAMS WERE REPORTING BACK TO
MR. AND MRS. FROG:
THE 'POSSUMS' REPORT –NO ALBERT!
THE FIELD MICE REPORT –NO ALBERT!
THE OWLS' REPORT –NO ALBERT!

Mientras todo le pasó a Albert, los grupos de la busqueda estuvieron informando a Sr. y Sra. Rana:

el informe de los 'possums'---no Albert! el informe de los ratones---no Albert! el informe de los buhos---no Albert!

THE CROWS' REPORT---NO ALBERT!
THE BATS' REPORT---NO ALBERT!

el informe de las comejas---no Albert!

El informe de los murciélagos---no Albert!

EVERYONE HAD BECOME TERRIBLY DISCOURAGED, AND THEIR SPIRITS WERE AS DARK AS THE NIGHT WHICH ENVELOPE THEM, AND TEARS OF SADNESS STREAMED DOWN THE CHEEKS OF ALL.

Todos hubian puestos teriblemente desanimado y sus espiritúis estuvieron tan obscuras como la noche de cual les enrodeó, y lagrimas de tristeza corrieron sobre las mejillas de todos.

It was now three in the morning, and Albert had been swimming for hours. He know he could not go on any long and, with that realizations said goodbye to the world as he sank below the surface, for what he knew was the last time, he thought of all the things he would never get to do, and he was very sad. Suddenly, that little voice in his brain cried out: "You are too young to die. Don't give up! And amazingly, Albert found the strength to swim back to the surface and try and again and again.

Ahora fue las tres de la mañana, y Albert hubo estado nadando horas. El supo que no pudiera seguir como asi y, con esa realizacion, despidió al mundo. Mientras el se sumergió abajo de la superficie la ultima vez, él pensó sobre todas las cosas nunca podria hacer. Y él estuvo muy triste. De repente, esa voz suave del profundo de su cerebro gritó.

"Eres demasiado joven a morir!!! Note dndas!!!"

Y asombrosamente, Albert encontró las fuerzas para nadar a la superficie y intentalo otra vez y otra vez y otra vez.

The night was long and the hours longer, but when the morning sun rose to greet the dawn, there was Albert sitting on a pad of Butter!

La noche fue larga y más largas las horas. Pero cuando el sol subió para saludar a la madrugada, alli hubo Albert sentado sobre una pad de mantequilla!

AND WITH A GREAT LEAP, ALBERT JUMPED OUT OF THE PAIL AND HURRIED HOME.

Y con un brinco grandisimo, Albert saltó afuera del cubo y se apurió al hogar.

When Albert appeared at his home, no one could believe their eyes! Everyone danced and sang, and tears of joy now washed away tears of grief. Albert's family was so thankful for this miracle. They invite all the inhabitants of the bog to a glorious celebration of life.

Cuando Albert apareció a la casa, nadie creó sus ojos! Todos bailaron y cantaron y unas lagrimas de gozo deslavaron las lagrimas de tristeza. La familia de Albert fue tan agradecidos para este milagro que ellos invitaron a todos los habitantes del pantano a una celebracion gloriosa de vida.

AND EVERYONE CAME. BUT NOT ALBERT. NOW WHERE WAS HE?

Y todos vinieron, pero no Albert. Donde está ahora?

ALBERT WAS FAST ASLEEP FOR HE HAD HAD A LONG HARD NIGHT AND WAS VERY, VERY, VERY TIRED.

Albert estuvo profundamente dormido porque le hubo pasado una noche larga y dificil y él estuvo muy, muy, muy cansado.

AND REMEMBER.

Entonces recuerdate.

No Matter how dire the straits,

No importa como tan extremo los estrechos,

Or perilous the circumstance,

o peligrosas las circunstancias,

OR PESSIMISTIC THE PROGNOSIS,

o pesimisto el pronóstico,

DON'T EVER STOP PADDLING.

Nunca deja de nadando

THE END

ABOUT THE AUTHOR

Dr. Jan Hahn was born in 1951 in Massachusetts and raised in Vineland, N.J. After graduating from Swarthmore College, he entered Mt. Sinai School of Medicine in New York City. Upon completing a family practice residency program in Galveston, Texas, he joined the Indian Health Service and worked for four years at Cherokee !HS Hospital in Cherokee, N.C. In 1984, he moved to Lenoir City, TN. where he practiced family medicine until his retirement in July, 2012.

In 2009, he returned to college to study English, and in 2011, he enrolled in Lincoln Memorial University's post-bac teacher licensure program. He is now certified to teach English 7-12.

In 1991, he started a domestic violence program, Crisis Center for Women-IVAS, and continues to be its chairman of the board.

This is his third book. The first one, entitled *Voices,* is a collection of poems describing many of the patients he has cared for during his thirty-five-year career in medicine. His second book is *A Gallimaufry*.

Dr. Hahn lives with his wife, Dr. Heather O'Brien, a veterinarian, and their seven horses, six dogs, twelve chickens, and one very contented rooster. His three daughters, Micah, Avital, and Mara are away at school.

ABOUT THE ARTIST

Ms. Tracy Foster is a native Tennessean. After graduating from University of Tennessee - Knoxville with a B.A. in art, she enrolled in Lincoln Memorial University's post-bac teacher licensure program. She intends to teach art in the public school system. She currently resides in Corryton with her fiancé and children.

ABOUT THE TRANSLATOR

Ms. Ashley Williams was born in Memphis, TN., the oldest of six. After graduating from the University of Tennessee - Knoxville with degrees in global studies, society, and culture and Spanish, she moved to Guatemala to work in an orphanage for a year. She currently resides in Knoxville.

www.ingramcontent.com/pod-product-compliance
Lightning Source LLC
Chambersburg PA
CBHW081001120626
46546CB00010B/2993